NATURE DETECTIVE

# Urban Wildlife

## A Photographic Guide

Victoria Munson

WAYLAND

First published in 2019 by Wayland
Copyright © Hodder and Stoughton, 2019

Wayland, an imprint of
Hachette Children's Group
Part of Hodder and Stoughton
Carmelite House
50 Victoria Embankment
London EC4Y 0DZ
An Hachette UK Company
www.hachette.co.uk
www.hachettechildrens.co.uk

Editor: Victoria Brooker
Designer: Elaine Wilkinson

ISBN: 978 1 5263 1212 9 (hbk)
ISBN: 978 1 5263 1213 6 (pbk)

Printed in China

Acknowledgements:
Shutterstock images: cover: Rudmer Zwerver (bat), aaltair (mallard), Emi (squirrel), Ian Thraves Photography (fox), Dom J (road); Title page; 6 Oligo; 8, 10 CreativeNature.nl; 9 Sandy Hedgepeth; 13 hadot 760; 14 karloss; 15 BeppeNob; 16, 17Martin Fowler; 18 Tompet; 20 Lostry7; 34 Volker Rauch; 34 inset Ziablik; 24 Ralf Neumann; 25 Daniel Prude; 26 Gl0ck; 27 Digoarpi; 28 inset berries Mageon; 29 Andy Rowland; 29 inset Martin Fowler; 30 LensTravel; 31 Sergey Uryadnikov; 32 top Rob Kemp; 32 bottom craigbirdphotos; 33 bottom Bogdan Boev; 34, 35 IbajaUsap; 36 Rob Kemp; 37 top Martin Fowler; 37 bottom Martin Spurny; 38 top Ainars Aunins; 38bAnatoliy Lukich; 39t Gucio_25; 39b pixel; 40 Peter Zijlstra; 41 Larsek; 42t Grant Glendinning; 42 Bjorn Stefanson; 43 Vitaly Ilyasov; 48 Kletr; 49 EMJAY SMITH; 50 Brian Maudsley; 51 Arto Hakola; 52 Sue Robinson; 53 Bildagentur Zoonar GmbH; 54 Mirvav; 55 Adam Edwards; 56 Hannu Rama; 57 artconcept; 58 alslutsky; 59 Florian Andronache; Istock: AntiMartina 19; 40 Bluefly06; 23 RelaxFoto.de; 28 mtreasure; 33 top Andrew Howe; 44 Derek Audette; 45 Iliuta Goean; 46 Roberto Zocchi; 47t &b rekemp; Corbis Dietmar Nill/Foto Natura/Minden Pictures/Corbis 7; Stephen Dalton/Minden Pictures/Corbis 11; Derek Middleton/FLPA/Minden Pictures/Corbis 12;

# Contents

# Be an urban nature detective!

To be a nature detective, you need to be observant, patient and quiet. Animals and insects scare easily and can by shy, so it might take time before you can spot them. Some animals are nocturnal, which means they are active at night.

## Spotting urban wildlife

You can see urban wildlife in villages, towns and cities. There is wildlife everywhere, from the plants growing in pavement cracks to trees in a churchyard and the insects buzzing past your head. You can be a nature detective in lots of different places, such as in your local park, alongside canals and rivers, or even just walking down the street. Look up, down and around and you'll be amazed at what you can see.

Colour pencils

Binoculars

Notebook

Waterproof jacket

These items might be useful when you're out and about spotting nature.

bushy tail

short ears

Eating nut

## Making notes

Once you've spotted some wildlife, use a notebook to write down or sketch some details about them. That way, if they're disturbed and fly or scurry away, then you have some details written down to help you identify them. You could add these to a scrapbook of your nature discoveries to make your own identification book of wildlife in your local area.

## Scientific names

Each species has its own scientific name. This name is the same around the world. Many also have their own common name, such as Blackbird or Daisy. The common name might be different in each country, or even within the same country. In Britain, for example, Rowan trees are also called Mountain Ash trees.

# Hedgehog

**Size:** 16–25 cm
**Scientific name:** *Erinaceus europaeus*
**Habitat:** Hedgerows, parks and gardens
**Food:** Beetles, worms and slugs
**Lifespan:** up to 5 years

Don't feed hedgehogs milk and bread. This will make them ill. Try unsalted peanuts or grated cheese.

Hedgehogs have light-brown tipped spikes on their round bodies. An adult hedgehog will have between 5–7,000 spines. They are mostly nocturnal, meaning that you will usually only see them at night. In about October, when the weather starts to turn colder, hedgehogs hibernate. They dig a small hole and cover themselves with leaves, either under hedges, in gardens or in woodland. They come out when the weather gets a bit warmer again around April.

Large, pointed
ears

# Fox

**Size:** 1–1.2 m
**Scientific name:** *Vulpes vulpes*
**Habitat:** Towns, woodland and farmland
**Food:** Mammals, birds and insects
**Lifespan:** 2–3 years in the wild

Foxes have pointed
ears and the same body
shape as a dog. They have reddy-
orange fur with a bushy, white-tipped tail.
Foxes are brilliant hunters, able to sprint and
jump. They live in dens hollowed out under a tree
root, or sometimes they will live in badger setts. Foxes
bury any food they don't eat to come back to later.

# Grey Squirrel

**Size:** 27 cm
**Scientific name:** *Sciurus carolinensis*
**Habitat:** Parks, gardens and woodland
**Food:** Seeds, acorns and nuts
**Lifespan:** 3–6 years

Large, bushy tail

Long claws

Grey Squirrels were introduced to Britain from North America in the nineteeth century and they are now Britain's most common squirrel. Squirrels are well known for burying food to eat later. Some food stores are dug up again after a few hours, while some are found a few months later. Grey Squirrels have very good memories and use landmarks and smell to find their stores again.

# Common Shrew

**Size:** 7.5 cm
**Scientific name:** *Sorex araneus*
**Habitat:** Hedgerows, meadows, marshes and woodland
**Food:** Insects, slugs, snails and worms
**Lifespan:** 2 years

The Common Shrew needs to eat every 2–3 hours.

As its name suggests, the Common Shrew is fairly common. It is recognisable by its long, narrow nose. The fur is silky brown and grey on the underside. Common Shrews are always on the move, looking for food. Listen out and sometimes you might hear their high-pitched squeaks.

Large, round
ears

# House Mouse

**Size:** 8–10 cm
**Scientific name:** *Mus musculus*
**Habitat:** Farmland and towns
**Food:** Cereals, seeds, vegetables
and fruit
**Lifespan:** 1–2 years

The House Mouse's grey-brown
fur and large ears makes it distinct
from other mice. House mice live near
humans and will eat crops and leftover food.
They are good climbers, jumpers and swimmers,
using their tail for balance. They are mostly nocturnal.

10

## Brown Rat

**Size:** 22–27 cm
**Scientific name:** *Rattus norvegicus*
**Habitat:** Urban areas
**Food:** Scraps of food
**Lifespan:** up to 18 months

Dark grey
fur

Rats have coarse brown
or dark grey fur, with lighter
coloured underparts and a thick, scaly
tail. They live in colonies in tunnels near
houses and eat food they find lying around.
Rats often groom each other and sleep together
in groups.

11

Look out for bats in June and July.

# Common Pipistrelle Bat

**Wingspan:** 20–23 cm
**Scientific name:** *Pipistrellus pipistrellus*
**Habitat:** Woodland, farmland and towns
**Food:** Insects
**Lifespan:** up to 16 years

One Pipistrelle Bat will eat up to 3,000 insects in one night.

These are the most common British bats
and they are also the smallest. They have dark-brown
to rusty coloured fur on their back, and yellowish-brown
fur on their underside. Their nose and ears are black. At dusk,
they come out of their roost, in lofts and buildings, to find food.
If you see one flying, it will have a jerky flight pattern. From mid-November
to April, they hibernate in building crevices, bat boxes, trees and cellars.

Daisies got their name from the words 'day's eye' because they close at night and open in the daytime.

# Common Daisy

**Scientific name:** *Bellis perennis*
**Height:** 4–12 cm
**Family:** Daisy
**Habitat:** Fields, meadows and gardens
**Flowers:** March to October

Daisies can be seen covering gardens and playing fields from early springtime. The thin, white petals can sometimes be tinged with pink. A large number of tiny florets crowd together to make the bright yellow button in the centre.

# Dandelion

**Scientific name:** *Taraxacum officinale*
**Height:** 5–40 cm
**Family:** Daisy
**Habitat:** Fields, roadsides and grassy places
**Flowers:** March to October

Dandelion leaves can be eaten in salads or used to make wine and tea.

Dandelions are familiar plants with their heads of bright yellow florets. In late summer, the florets develop into 'dandelion clocks'. These are clusters of small, singled-seeded fruits, each with a tuft of white hairs at the tip. The hairs spread the seeds in the wind like a parachute.

# Meadow Buttercup

**Scientific name:** *Ranunculus acris*
**Height:** up to 1 m
**Family:** Buttercup
**Habitat:** Gardens, fields and meadows
**Flowers:** May to September

Meadow Buttercups are one
of the tallest types of buttercup.
They are recognisable by their five bright-
yellow, shiny petals and their long, upright
stem, surrounded by whorls of thin, pointed green
leaves. They have smooth, round stalks.

15

# White Clover

**Scientific name:** *Trifolium repens*
**Height:** up to 30 cm
**Family:** Pea
**Habitat:** Gardens, fields and meadows
**Flowers:** May to October

Red Clover looks the same as White Clover but with red petals.

This very common low-growing plant is often found growing near to daisies, buttercups and dandelions. Clover has clusters of tiny white, or pinkish, flowers on thin, upright stalks. The leaves have three round leaflets, marked with a pale 'v' shape.

# Stinging Nettle

**Scientific name:** *Urtica dioica*
**Height:** 30–150 cm
**Family:** Nettle
**Habitat:** Gardens and fields
**Flowers:** June to September

These common weeds are well-known to all. The dark green, heart-shaped, toothed leaves can give a nasty sting, as can the sharp hairs on the stem. However, they don't sting insects and many butterflies, such as the Peacock and the Red Admiral, lay eggs on them. The hatched caterpillars then eat the nettle leaves.

Cooked nettles can be added to soups, stews and tea.

# White Deadnettle

**Scientific name:** *Lamium album*
**Height:** 20–60 cm
**Family:** Mint
**Habitat:** Hedges, roadsides and waste ground
**Flowers:** May to December

White Deadnettles look very
similar to Stinging Nettles, but
unlike Stinging Nettles, they don't sting and are
recognisable by the creamy white flowers at the top of
square stems. The flowers have an unusual curved hood
and a lip. Heart-shaped, toothed leaves are covered in fine hair.
Red Deadnettle looks the same as White Deadnettle but have
purplish-pink flowers.

# Field Bindweed

**Latin name:** *Convolvulus arvensis*
**Height:** 20–75 cm
**Family:** Bindweed
**Habitat:** Fields, gardens and waste ground
**Flowers:** June to September

This pretty flower is in fact a pest because it has long roots that are hard to get rid of. The roots can stretch up to 2 metres underground. Its thin, twisty stem wraps itself tightly around other plants for support. Flowers can be pale pink, white, or pink and white-striped and they smell sweet. Leaves are grey-green, pointed ovals.

# Common Mallow

**Scientific name:** *Malva sylvestris*
**Height:** 45–90 cm
**Family:** Mallow
**Habitat:** Roadsides and grassy areas
**Flowers:** June to October

Common Mallow have notched, pink petals with dark purple
veins. The strong, thick stalk is hairy. Leaves are large
and dark green with five lobes. The leaves look crinkly when
the plant is young. Mallow can survive without water for a long time.

The ancient Romans used to grow Mallow for food and medicine.

# Cow Parsley

**Scientific name:** *Anthriscus sylvestris*
**Height:** 60–100 cm
**Family:** Carrot
**Habitat:** Hedgerows, fields, roadside verges
**Flowers:** April to June

Cow Parsley is called 'Queen Anne's Lace' after its frilly leaves.

These tall plants have clusters of white flowers on flat flower heads. Many branches of flower heads come from one tall stem, resembling the spokes of an umbrella. The leaves are finely divided into many pairs of toothed leaflets, so they look rather fern-like.

# Horse Chestnut

**Scientific name:** *Aesculus hippocastanum*
**Height:** up to 40 metres
**Life span:** up to 300 years

In winter, look out for large, brown-red sticky buds.

These large trees are better-known as 'conker trees'. In summer, Horse Chestnuts are covered in large spikes of white, or pale pink, flowers. The spiny fruits that grow in autumn contain seeds called conkers. Each leaf is made up of 5–7 long leaflets. The greyish-green bark has large flakes breaking from it. Horse Chestnuts are not edible.

# London Plane

**Scientific name:** *Platanus x hispanica*
**Height:** up to 35 metres
**Life span:** up to 500 years

seed balls

Most often found in towns and cities, London Plane trees are said to make up half of the trees in London. They have large glossy leaves about 10 cm wide, with noticeable veins. As the trunk grows, its grey bark continually flakes off revealing a creamy yellow and light brown bark beneath. Through winter, you can see dried brown seed balls hanging from the branches. Seeds are released from these in spring.

# Silver Birch

**Scientific name:** *Betula pendula*
**Height:** up to 30 metres
**Life span:** 80–150 years

catkins

Silver Birch gets its name from its silver-coloured trunk. The bark peels off in strips leaving dark marks. Heart-shaped leaves have toothed edges. Male catkins droop downwards and are about 3 cm long. Female catkins are smaller and upright.

# Common Lime

**Scientific name:** *Tilia x europaea*
**Height:** up to 40 metres
**Life span:** up to 400 years

The Common Lime has broad, heart-shaped leaves with toothed edges. You can usually find small tufts of creamy white hair in the leaf veins. Limes attract greenfly and blackfly that feed on the leaves making them sticky. Sweet-smelling, yellow-white flowers appear in July and turn into small seed balls. Suckers grow from the base of the tree.

# Small Leaved Lime

**Scientific name:** *Tilia cordata*
**Height:** up to 30 metres
**Life span:** over 500 years

Lime flowers are used for herbal tea.

Small Leaved Limes are often planted in residential areas, because of their sweet-smelling flowers. The flowers are white-yellow and hang in clusters on a long stalk. Fruits are oval with pointed tips. The hairless leaves are heart-shaped, with a pointed tip at the end.

# Large Leaved Lime

**Scientific name:** *Tilia platyphyllos*
**Height:** up to 35 metres
**Life span:** over 1,000 years

This tall tree has, as its name suggests, larger leaves than the Small Leaved Lime. The leaves have a hairy stalk and the bark is dark brown. Fruits are rounded and smooth with pointed tips. This Lime doesn't produce suckers from the base of the tree.

# Hawthorn

**Scientific name:** *Crataegus monogyna*
**Height:** 5–12 metres
**Life span:** up to 250 years

Hawthorn is also called the 'May tree' because it is in full flower throughout May.

Hawthorn can grow as a shrub, hedge or small tree. The stems of a young hawthorn are covered in sharp thorns. The bark is brown and often covered in green algae. Its leaves are small and deeply-lobed. White flowers appear in spring. In autumn, the flowers turn into dark red berries called 'haws'. These can be used in jams and jellies.

# Yew

**Scientific name:** *Taxus baccata*
**Height:** up to 30 metres
**Life span:** over 1,000 years

Yew trees are often found in graveyards. They have a distinctive red flaky bark. The leaves are needle-like, long and narrow. In spring, seeds sit in a bright-red, fleshy cup.

Yew leaves and berries are extremely poisonous to humans.

# Holly

**Scientific name:** *Ilex aquifolium*
**Height:** up to 25 metres
**Life span:** up to 300 years

Holly berries are poisonous for humans.

Evergreen Holly trees have tough, spiky leaves. The spikes are to stop animals from eating them. Its bark is silver-grey. In spring, Holly has small, four-petalled, white flowers. Bright red berries in autumn attract many birds.

**Bright orange beak**

# Blackbird

**Size:** 25 cm
**Scientific name:** *Turdus merula*
**Family:** Thrushes
**Habitat:** Gardens and woodland
**Food:** Insects, fruit and berries
**Life span:** up to 5 years

Blackbirds like to eat berries and fruit. Try leaving out old or fallen apples to attract them to your garden.

Male Blackbirds are black with a bright yellowy-orange beak and yellow rings around their eyes. Females and their young are dark brown with a speckled throat. They feed on worms and can be seen hopping across gardens. Look out for them singing loudly from the top of a high perch. The male Blackbird has a beautiful song. It sings all through the breeding season.

# House Sparrow

**Size:** 14–15 cm
**Scientific name:** *Passer domesticus*
**Family:** Sparrows
**Habitat:** Towns and cities, farms
**Food:** Seeds, scraps and insects
**Life span:** 2–5 years

The House Sparrow is one of the most familiar small birds in Britain. The male has a grey crown, underside and rump, and a black bib. Its brown back is streaked with black and it has a white bar on its wings. The female House Sparrow is much plainer than the male, without the black markings.

# Robin

**Size:** 14 cm
**Scientific name:** *Erithacus rubecula*
**Family:** Chats and thrushes
**Habitat:** Parks, gardens, woodland and hedgerows
**Food:** Worms, seeds, fruit and insects
**Life span:** 3–5 years

Robins are easily recognised by their orange-red breast, brown back and rounded shape. Males and females look alike. Their young have a dark brown, speckled plumage. Robins sing all year round.

In winter, Robins puff up their feathers to keep warm.

# Song Thrush

**Size:** 22 cm
**Scientific name:** *Turdus philomelos*
**Family:** Thrushes
**Habitat:** Parks, gardens, woodland and hedgerows
**Food:** Worms, slugs, insects, fruit and berries
**Life span:** up to 5 years

The Song Thrush is pale brown with a cream-coloured breast flecked with dark-brown spots. It is slightly smaller than a Blackbird. When it is in flight, you can see its wings are slightly orange underneath. Its spots are heart-shaped.

# Mistle Thrush

**Size:** 27 cm
**Scientific name:** *Turdus viscivorus*
**Family:** Thrushes
**Habitat:** Parks, gardens, woodland and hedgerows
**Food:** Worms, slugs, insects, fruit and berries
**Life span:** 5–10 years

The Mistle Thrush is bigger than both the Song Thrush and the Blackbird. You can tell the two thrushes apart because Mistle Thrushes are bigger and they do not have the orange colouring beneath their wings. Their spots are wider and more defined than a Song Thrush's.

Watch for flocks in July and August.

# Great Tit

**Size:** 14 cm
**Scientific name:** *Parus major*
**Family:** Tits
**Habitat:** Gardens, woodland and fields
**Food:** Insects, seeds and nuts
**Life span:** 2–3 years

Great Tits have a clutch of 5–11 eggs in April or May.

The Great Tit is the largest member of the tit family. It has a distinctive black stripe down its yellow breast and a glossy black head. Great Tits are common visitors to bird tables and garden feeders.

Blue cap

Yellow breast

# Blue Tit

**Size:** 11.5 cm
**Scientific name:** *Cyanistes caeruleus*
**Family:** Tits
**Habitat:** Gardens, parks and woodland
**Food:** Insects, caterpillars, seeds and nuts
**Life span:** 2–3 years

Blue Tits are very
colourful, lively birds.
They have a yellow breast
with blue wings and a blue cap.
A pair of Blue Tits can collect hundreds
of caterpillars each day to feed their young.
By the time Blue Tit chicks fly the nest, they
may have eaten up to 10,000 caterpillars.

# Collared Dove

**Size:** 31–33 cm
**Scientific name:** *Streptopelia decaocto*
**Family:** Pigeons and doves
**Habitat:** Gardens and parks
**Food:** Seeds and grain
**Life span:** up to 10 years

Black collar

Collared Doves are not very good nest makers. Sometimes chicks fall through the branches of the nest.

Collared Doves
are recognisable
because of the black 'collar' on
their neck and their pinkish plumage.
They have deep red eyes and reddish feet.
Listen for their 'coo-COO-coo' call.

White patch

# Woodpigeon

**Size:** 41 cm
**Scientific name:** *Columba palumbus*
**Family:** Pigeons and doves
**Habitat:** Fields, parks and gardens
**Food:** Crops, buds, shoots, berries, seeds and nuts.
**Life span:** up to 10 years

Woodpigeons are the largest and most common of our pigeons. They are grey and have white bars on their wings, which are easier to see when the pigeon is flying. They also have white patches on the sides of their neck. In winter, they can often be found in huge flocks.

Green neck

# Feral Pigeon

**Size:** 32 cm
**Scientific name:** *Columba livia*
**Family:** Pigeons and doves
**Habitat:** Parks and gardens, fields, woodland,
**Food:** Seeds and cereals
**Life span:** up to 10 years

This common city bird comes in many different shades, from black to white, grey or brown. They usually have a green or purple sheen on their neck and black wing bars.

# Carrion Crow

**Size:** 46 cm
**Scientific name:** *Corvus corone*
**Family:** Crows
**Habitat:** Parks, roadsides and woodland
**Food:** Carrion, insects, worms, seeds, fruit and scraps
**Life span:** 5–10 years

Carrion Crows are usually seen alone or in pairs. They are completely black with a powerful beak. They are intelligent, adaptable and can live almost anywhere. Carrion Crows hop rather than walk.

# Magpie

**Size:** 46 cm
**Scientific name:** *Pica pica*
**Family:** Crows
**Habitat:** Gardens and parks
**Food:** Insects, plants, carrion, small birds and eggs
**Life span:** 10–15 years

Magpies are as big as Crows,
but have distinctive black and white plumage.
Up close you can see a green gloss on the tail. They are usually seen in pairs but sometimes flock together in groups of 20–40 to nest.

**Black cap**

# Jackdaw

**Size:** 33–34 cm
**Scientific name:** *Corvus monedula*
**Family:** Crows
**Habitat:** Parks, gardens, fields, and woodland,
**Food:** Insects, seeds and scraps
**Life span:** 5–10 years

The Jackdaw is the smallest crow commonly seen in Britain. It looks black all over, but has a grey neck and cheeks. During the winter, Jackdaws often join Rooks to make large flocks. They have a distinctive 'jack jack' call.

# Rook

**Size:** 44–46 cm
**Scientific name:** *Corvus frugilegus*
**Family:** Crows
**Habitat:** Farmland and woodland
**Food:** Worms, grains and insects
**Life span:** 5–10 years

Rooks are slightly smaller than the Carrion Crow and look like they're wearing 'baggy trousers'. You usually see Rooks in large flocks and they nest in colonies (rookeries) at the top of tall trees.

# Starling

**Size:** 21 cm
**Scientific name:** *Sturnus vulgaris*
**Family:** Starlings
**Habitat:** Towns and cities, farms
**Food:** Insects and fruit
**Life span:** up to 5 years

Purple-green sheen on wing

Short tail

Starlings mimic the sounds of other birds, mammals and even telephones and car alarms!

Starlings are one of Britain's most common garden birds. A Starling looks black from a distance, but up close it has a green or purple sheen on its wing. Starlings live in large flocks and can be very noisy when grouped together.

# Ring-necked Parakeet

**Size:** 39–43 cm
**Scientific name:** *Psittacula krameri*
**Family:** Parrots
**Habitat:** Parks and gardens
**Food:** Fruit, berries, nuts and seeds
**Life span:** 20–30 years

Red hooked bill

Long tail

This type of Parakeet escaped from collections near London and bred in the wild. They can now be found across the south-east of England. They are unmistakable with their green bodies, long tails and red bills. Parakeets often form large flocks and can be very noisy!

# Chaffinch

**Size:** 15 cm
**Scientific name:** *Fringilla coelebs*
**Family:** Finches
**Habitat:** Parks, gardens, woodland and hedgerows
**Food:** Insects and seeds
**Life span:** 2–5 years

Female Chaffinch

Listen out for Chaffinches singing in early spring.

Male Chaffinch

The male Chaffinch is one of Britain's most colourful birds. Males have a pinky face and breast and a blue-grey crown. Females are sandy brown. Both male and female Chaffinches have black and white wings, and a green rump. During the winter, Chaffinches often group together in large flocks on the edges of woodland, where they search for seeds to eat.

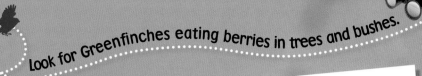
Look for Greenfinches eating berries in trees and bushes.

# Greenfinch

**Size:** 15 cm
**Scientific name:** *Carduelis chloris*
**Family:** Finches
**Habitat:** Parks and gardens
**Food:** Seeds, berries and insects
**Life span:** 2–3 years

**Yellow on wing**

The Greenfinch is a popular
garden visitor. The male Greenfinch's
plumage is mostly yellow and green with
bits of grey. Its forked tail has a dark tip. Females
can get confused for sparrows, but when they fly off
you'll see a flicker of yellow in their tail and wings.

# Common Gull

**Size:** 55–60 cm
**Scientific name:** *Larus canus*
**Family:** Gulls
**Habitat:** Towns and parks, coasts and marshes,
**Food:** Fish, carrion and insects
**Life span:** Up to 10 years

Common Gulls have grey
wings, a black tail with white
bars, a white head and body, and a
yellow beak. In winter (pictured) their
white head is specked with grey.

# Mute Swan

Size: 140–160 cm
Scientific name: *Cygnus olor*
Family: Swans, ducks and geese
Habitat: Rivers, ponds and lakes
Food: Water plants, insects and snails
Life span: 15–20 years

Young swans are called cygnets.

Mute Swans are Britain's largest bird. They are white with a long 's'-shaped neck and an orange bill with a black tip. They have a lump at the top of their beak. Swans can get angry and will hiss and flap their wings. A male swan is called a 'cob'; a female is called a 'pen'.

# Mallard

**Size:** 50–65 cm
**Scientific name:** *Anas platyrhynchos*
**Family:** Swans, ducks and geese
**Habitat:** Ponds, rivers and lakes
**Food:** Seeds, acorns and berries,
plants, insects and shellfish.
**Life span:** 15–25 years

Mallards have a clutch of 9–13 eggs.

Female

Male

The Mallard is the most
common type of duck in Britain.
The male Mallard has a green head,
a white ring around its neck, a brown
breast and a pale grey back. The female
Mallard is speckled brown.

# Moorhen

**Size:** 32–35 cm
**Scientific name:** *Gallinula chloropus*
**Family:** Swans, ducks and geese
**Habitat:** Ponds, rivers and lakes
**Food:** Water plants, seeds, fruit, grasses, insects, snails, worms and small fish
**Life span:** up to 15 years

Moorhens are black, with a red forehead and a yellow-tipped red beak. They have long green toes and white along their wings and tail.

# Coot

**Size:** 36–38 cm
**Scientific name:** *Fulica atra*
**Family:** Rails
**Habitat:** Ponds, rivers and lakes
**Food:** Vegetation, snails and insect larvae
**Life span:** up to 15 years

Coots and Moorhens can often be seen together, but Coots are slightly larger and have a white forehead and beak.

 Coots can run along the surface of water.

# Honey Bee

**Scientific name:** *Apis mellifera*
**Size:** 1.6 cm
**Habitat:** Gardens, parks, woodland

Honey Bees have slightly hairy, brown-black bodies with orangey-yellow bands and large black eyes. They will sting when they feel threatened, but once they have stung they die, unlike Common Wasps who can sting again and again. Honey Bees live together in large numbers in nests.

# Red-tailed Bumblebee

Scientific name: *Bombus lapidarius*
Size: 2.3 cm
Habitat: Gardens, farmland, woodland
and hedgerows

Red-tailed Bumblebees are very common bumblebees.
The females are large black bees with a red tail. Males are smaller
than females and have two yellow bands on the thorax and one
at the base of the abdomen. They build nests in walls, in straw in
stables, or in abandoned birds' nests. Look for them feeding on
daisies, dandelions and thistles.

# Seven-spot Ladybird

**Scientific name:** *Coccinella 7-punctata*
**Size:** up to 6 mm
**Habitat:** Gardens, parks and woodland

Ladybirds can beat their wings 85 times per second.

This small, round beetle has bright-red wing cases dotted with seven black spots. The bright colour warns predators that it tastes horrible. If a ladybird thinks it is about to be attacked, it will produce small blobs of yellow blood from its legs as a warning. In summer, female ladybirds lay clusters of eggs on leaves. The eggs hatch into small black larvae. The larvae have spiky grey-blue skin with yellow spots. The larvae turn into pupae, which become adult ladybirds in a couple of weeks.

# Black Garden Ant

**Scientific name:** *Lasius niger*
**Size:** up to 0.5 cm
**Habitat:** Gardens, parks, woodlands

One Black Ant colony can contain more than 5,000 ants.

Black Garden Ants live together in huge colonies on the ground. Worker Black Ants are wingless, brown-black females that cannot breed. Each colony has one or two queen ants that are much larger than worker ants. Male ants are smaller than females and have wings.

# Pond Skater

**Scientific name:** *Gerris lacustris*
**Size:** 1.5 cm
**Habitat:** Ponds and lakes

Pond Skaters are also known as 'Magic Bugs', 'Water Striders' and 'Jesus Bugs'.

Pond Skaters are small bugs with a brownish-black, narrow body. They have tiny hairs on their feet that repel water and allow them to 'skate' on the surface of ponds. They use their middle pair of legs to move themselves forwards with a rowing or jumping motion, and they use their rear pair of legs to steer left or right. The front pair of legs is used to catch and hold insects to eat.

# Crane Fly

**Scientific name:** *Tipula paludosa*
**Size:** 2 cm
**Habitat:** Gardens, parks and grassy areas

Crane Flies have long, grey-brown bodies and long legs, which give them their nickname 'Daddy-Long-Legs'. Their two wings are thin and translucent. Crane Flies are attracted by lights, which is why they often fly into houses in the evening. They sometimes lose a leg trying to escape from a predator, but they can still survive without one or two legs.

# Large White

Large Whites are also known as 'Cabbage Whites'.

**Scientific name:** *Pieris brassicae*
**Wingspan:** 6 cm
**Habitat:** Gardens, parks and farmland
**Family:** Whites and yellows

Large White butterflies look very similar to Small Whites, but Large Whites are, as the name gives away, much larger and their black markings are much darker. Females have two black spots while the males have no spots. Caterpillars are grey-green and mottled with black spots and yellow stripes. They stay as pupae through winter and adults emerge in spring. The caterpillars love to feed on cabbages, so they are not popular with farmers.

# Small White

**Scientific name:** *Pieris rapae*
**Wingspan:** 5 cm
**Family:** Whites and yellows
**Habitat:** Gardens, parks and farmland

One of the most common butterflies in Britain, the Small White is, as its name suggests, small and white. The females have two black spots and a black streak on the forewings. Males also have two black spots, but the second of these spots is much lighter. Small White caterpillars are a pest because they like to feed on cabbages and Brussels sprouts.

# Peacock

**Scientific name:** *Inachis io*
**Wingspan:** 6.5–7.5 cm
**Habitat:** Gardens, fields and orchards
**Family:** Nymphalids

Peacock caterpillars like to eat nettles.

This common garden butterfly has striking yellow and blue eyespots on the tip of each wing. These spots give the butterfly its name because they look like the markings on a peacock bird. In winter, Peacock butterflies hibernate in hollow trees and sheds.

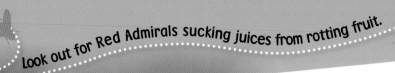

Look out for Red Admirals sucking juices from rotting fruit.

# Red Admiral

**Scientific name:** *Vanessa atalanta*
**Wingspan:** 5.5–6 cm
**Habitat:** most habitats
**Family:** Nymphalids

These striking red and black butterflies are common visitors to gardens. They have bars of red on their fore and hindwings, with white spots on the tips of their forewings. The underside of their wings is a dark brown and black, which provides good camouflage when they rest on tree bark.

# Small Tortoiseshell

Scientific name: *Aglais urticae*
Wingspan: 4.5–6.2 cm
Habitat: Woodland, grassland, gardens, city centres
Family: Nymphalids

Small Tortoiseshell butterflies are bright orange with black and yellow bars on their forewings and black arches filled with blue edging on all four wings. Female Tortoiseshells can lay 80–100 eggs on the underside of nettle leaves.

The Small Tortoiseshell is one of the first butterflies to appear in spring.

# Common Earwig

**Scientific name:** *Forficula auricularia*
**Size:** 1.3–1.8 cm
**Habitat:** Gardens, parks and woodland

Earwigs got their name because of their ear-shaped wings.

Common Earwigs are easy to identify because they have prominent pincers at the rear end of their body. Male Earwigs have a pair of long curved pincers, while female pincers are smaller and straighter. Both have shiny brown bodies. Although they have wings, it is rare to see Common Earwigs flying. They are mostly nocturnal, coming out at night to feed.

# Further information

## Places to visit

National Trust
**www.nationaltrust.org.uk/visit/places/find-a-place-to-visit**

Protecting a range of spaces and places in England, Wales and Northern Ireland, the National Trust takes care of forests, woods, fens, beaches, farmland, moorland and nature reserves as well as historic houses and gardens. Find somewhere new to visit in your local area or further afield.

The Wildlife Trusts
**www.wildlifetrusts.org/visit**
Find a nature reserve near you

**National Wildflower Centre www.nwc.org.uk**
The National Wildflower Centre aims to raise awareness of the importance of wildflowers to the environment. It has seasonal displays and encourages people to create their own wildflower areas.

**www.rspb.org.uk/reserves**
Find out about more than 150 RSPB nature reserves where you can watch wildlife

# Useful websites

**www.butterfly-conservation.org/679/a-z-of-butterflies.html**
The Butterfly Conservation website has an excellent A-Z of butterflies and moths. Find out how to register for the Big Butterfly Count.

**www.mammal.org.uk**
Information and downloadable factsheets on all British mammals

**www.nhm.ac.uk/take-part/identify-nature.html**
The Natural History Museum has several identification guides

**www.plantlife.org.uk/wild_plants/plant_species/**
An A-Z of wild flowers with descriptions and photographs

**www.rspb.org.uk**
Information on every bird, including a bird identifier. Find out how to register for the Big Garden Birdwatch.

**www.wildlifetrusts.org/wildlife/species-explorer**
The Wildlife Trusts species explorer page gives you photographs and descriptions of British animals, fish, amphibians and birds

**www.woodlandtrust.org.uk/learn/british-trees**
Identification guides to native and non-native British trees, including sections on places to visit

# Glossary

**abdomen** the back part of an insect, joined to the thorax

**bar** a patch of colour on a bird

**bark** the outside of a tree's trunk

**beak** the hard mouth part of a bird

**belly** the part of a bird's body between its breast and its tail

**breast** the part of a bird's body between its throat and belly

**camouflage** colours on an animal's body that blend with the background, making it difficult to spot

**catkins** petalless flowers that hang from trees and are usually pollinated by the wind

**clutch** a group of eggs laid at one time

**colonies** groups of the same animal that all live together

**crown** the top part of a bird's head

**family** a grouping of species that are similar

**flock** a group of birds

**floret** small flowers

**flower head** a cluster of small flowers that often look like one flower

**forewing** the front, or forward, wing of an insect

**fruit** the part of a plant that holds the seeds

**habitat** the place where a plant or an animal lives in the wild

**hibernate** to spend winter sleeping

**hindwing** the back, or backward, wing of an insect

**leaflet** a small, separate part of a leaf

**native** an animal, tree or plant that grows naturally in an area

**nocturnal** active at night

**petals** the showy part of the flower which attract insects

**plumage** a bird's feathers

**predator** an animal that hunts and eats other animals

**roost** a place where birds or bats rest

**rump** the area of a bird's body above its tail

**species** one of the groups into which trees, plants and other living things are divided

**suckers** a new branch that grows from the base of a tree

**thorax** the middle part of the body of an insect – the legs and wings are attached to the thorax

**translucent** partly see-through

**whorls** rings of leaves around the stem of a plant

# Index

Become a nature detective and discover how to identify common British wildlife with these fantastic titles:

9780750283410

9781526301574

9781526301185

9780750293211

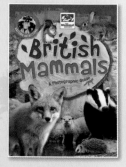

9780750283427

9780750293235

9780750293259

9780750293273

Let's investigate!